BRITAIN IN OLD PHO

BRENTWOOD, SHENFIELD & WARLEY

W.E. Crow's Tea Rooms at 37 High Street, 1912. The frontage is painted white – a style of the time which drew attention to the business from passing trade. Note Fitch's Cab Yard on the right: two taxi businesses still trade from similar yards.

BRITAIN IN OLD PHOTOGRAPHS

BRENTWOOD, SHENFIELD & WARLEY

DON HEWSON

SUTTON PUBLISHING LIMITED

Sutton Publishing Limited
Phoenix Mill · Thrupp · Stroud
Gloucestershire · GL5 2BU

First published 1997

Copyright © Don Hewson, 1997

Cover photographs: *front*: A smart couple
outside their villa in Crescent Road; *back*:
Amateur dramatics in Brentwood, 1930s.

British Library Cataloguing in Publication Data
A catalogue record for this book is available from the
British Library.

ISBN 0-7509-1299-5

Typeset in 10/12 Perpetua.
Typesetting and origination by
Sutton Publishing Limited.
Printed in Great Britain by
Ebenezer Baylis, Worcester.

Title Page: Duchess of York (later Queen Elizabeth) at the Child Haven.

G.A. Lipton in his butcher's delivery cart. Is the boy his son?

CONTENTS

INTRODUCTION

Brentwood is first mentioned in 1176 but until the late seventeenth century did not even have a vestry of its own to govern the town, being merely a part of the Parish of South Weald. It then became a hamlet and the first recorded vestry meeting to choose officials took place on 25 March 1695. Those elected were Robert Carter (a blacksmith) as Churchwarden (to represent Brentwood's interests at the South Weald vestry, who continued to levy rates from Brentwood), John Holmes and Richard Meeter as Overseers of the Poor, William Lambe as innkeeper, Alexander Bridges, John Cooke and William Poole as Constables, Jonathan Pope, a tailor, and Thomas Cole as Ale Connors, Isaac Hayward, a cordwainer, as Sidesman. A bit later in the year the meeting elected two Surveyors of the Highways and then in 1698 two Leather Sealers. The makeup of the vestry and descriptions of their duties give an insight into the vigorous life and work of old Brentwood. The Churchwarden, for instance, with his South Weald counterpart, was responsible for such diverse duties as the maintenance of the church, the guarding of the ancient boundaries of the parish by perambulation, the destruction of vermin and the relief of vagrants! The Overseers of the Poor, a connected office, seem to have had a full time job of their own, which was correspondingly unpopular. Overseers under the Settlement Laws of the time were responsible for the poor, and had to maintain a house for them to live in, provide work for them to do and also provide small pensions and relief in kind. They also spent a great deal of time keeping poor people who might become chargeable to the rates out of the town or removing to their home parishes those who had managed to enter the town. In one typical instance in 1737, Mr Foster, a Brentwood overseer, went to Kendal, a trip which took twenty-four days on the dreadful roads of that time; his expenses were 48s, a very large sum for the day. His mission had been to persuade the churchwardens of that town at the other end of England to take responsibility for Edmund Beck, who had tried to get himself maintained at Brentwood's expense.

An ancient earthworks in Sandpit Lane, South Weald, would seem to be the work of some of the earliest of primitive inhabitants of Brentwood. Roman relics have occasionally surfaced in the district. A well-preserved gold ring bearing a Christian Chi-Rho monogram was found near Hillside Walk in 1948. The Roman road was constructed in a straight line from Gallows Corner, Romford, passing through the parish boundary, up Brook Street Hill and through what is now Brentwood High Street. It is unlikely that there was any Roman settlement in Brentwood, thickly wooded as the area was on either side – only the sections alongside the road being cleared by the road builders to prevent a surprise ambush. However, a Roman posting station lay at Hare Street near Romford, not far to the south, and considerable traffic passed along the road at certain times on its way to the important Roman centres of Chelmsford and Colchester and the coast. The road was then practically abandoned in the Dark Ages, only coming strongly back in to use in late Norman times with the rise of new trade and commerce in England. Many important people travelled along its length from that time forward – kings, queens, notables and a host of others who sometimes chronicled their experiences of travel and of Brentwood. These include the rebel forces in the Peasants Revolt of 1388 and the diarists Evelyn and Pepys, as well as Doctor Johnson. Pepys' musician and secretary C. Morelli wrote to his master from Brentwood, saying that he was lodged with pleasant people and that the air was purer than that of London. In April 1681, while Pepys was ill in London, Morelli wrote to say that if his illness persisted there was a man in Brentwood who could cure him 'with sympathetical power'. All that was required was for Pepys to send 'the pearinghs of the nailes of both your hands and foots and three locks of hair on the top of your crown – I hope with the grace of God it will cure you'.

John Evelyn had a short connection with the district during the Civil War, purchasing the manor of Great Warley on 12 March 1649, but selling it again after only a few years in September 1655, complaining that 'the taxes are so intollerable that they eate up the rents etc., surcharged as that county has been during our unnatural war.'

From the mid-nineteenth century and the advent of the railway the town began to acquire population and housing, although for many years there was a decline in horse traffic on the Great Essex Road through it. The arrival of the motor car so changed things that a bypass constructed in the 1960s now takes traffic past the town, but not noticeably giving much relief to traffic congestion within its borders.

The Norman door at South Weald church, 1904. As Pevsner said: 'A large church in a fine position . . . with a surprisingly big west tower of *c*. 1500, ashlar-faced, with angle buttresses, battlements and a higher stair turret'. The south and east walls of the medieval church behind survive to form part of a Teulon designed rebuilding of 1868.

HISTORIC HIGHWAY

The Golden Fleece Inn and Brook Street Hill, 1906. A very old building and an inn for several centuries, the Golden Fleece was a courthouse in medieval times. It is also supposed to have been a monastic building: the ghost of a red-eyed monk has manifested itself from time to time within the inn and even in the Close behind. Pots, pans and glasses have in the past moved without explanation in the bars and kitchen.

Putwell Bridge Farm on the far western boundary of Brentwood, 1963. Just past this spot the old Roman road begins the ascent to the town.

Looking down Spital Lane, Brook Street, 1910. The name comes from there having been a leper hospital located here in medieval times, one of many on the great highroads of England. It is described in a 1553 document as 'le Spytle in Brokestrete'.

The old St Thomas à Becket Chapel remains, enclosed in their distinctive railings, 1904. The ruins consist of parts of the north and west walls, and the stump of the north-west tower, dating from the fourteenth century.

Part of the chapel ruins in the 1950s. It was founded in 1221, and was still being repaired in 1830, but shortly afterwards a new church was built. For a time the chapel became the Boys' National Schoolroom.

The Hunter Memorial commemorates the martyrdom of a young Brentwoodian who in the reign of Mary I refused to compromise about his beliefs and was burned at the stake (see page 18).

Until the construction of the Brentwood bypass this toll house, seen here in 1963, stood on the old Essex Road at the London end, beyond Brook Street. An earlier road improvement scheme had set up toll roads and houses to collect the money to pay for the first systematic road upkeep since the Romans. An Act of

1721 created the 'Middlesex and Essex Trust for Repairing the Highways from Stones End at Whitechapel . . . to Shenfield'.

Edward Lamb's bequest house, High Street, 1891. The rents from houses such as these paid for charitable works, for example almshouses and winter coal for the elderly poor.

Great Stompfords farmhouse, a piece of old England drawn by Bamford in 1891. This was in Back Street (Hart Street today), and its farmlands stretched away towards Little Warley and the station area.

The remains of the old elm tree commemorating William Hunter's martyrdom, 1920s. This old tree, outside Brentwood School in Ingrave Road, was replaced by an oak in 1936.

The lower part of the Brentwood Public School buildings in Ingrave Road. Founded by Antony Browne, a lawyer in the service of the Crown in the sixteenth century, the buildings date from many periods, including the Georgian and Victorian.

The older buildings of Brentwood School originated in 1568; parts of the outer structure survive. On the right is the school chapel, and outside the walls is the railed-off stump of the martyr's tree.

A TALE OF INNS

The High Street, c. 1910. The Swan Inn is on the left: it still exists in a rebuilt version. The sign of the Bell Inn on the right is first heard of in 1453, when William Boleyn was paid for painting the sign and John Reynold, blacksmith, for furnishing iron and nails. Inns in Brentwood are listed for various reasons in documents over the centuries. In the nineteenth century nineteen inns existed in the High Street. Like the Bell many ceased to exist – for example, the Star, the Jolly Baker, the Crown, the Welcome Stranger and the King's Head – by the twentieth century. Others, for example the Yorkshire Grey, the Lion and Lamb and the White Horse, have closed fairly recently, though the motifs of the Lion and Lamb still decorate its former premises – now W.H. Smith's. These hostelries were well patronized during the eighteenth and nineteenth centuries, first by the travellers on the coaches and stage wagons and later by the soldiers from Warley Barracks, who could number anything up to a couple of thousand.

Here we see the Swan Inn on both sides of a passageway, 1905. The Swan name first appears in 1783, having previously been the Gun and earlier still the Argent. In the past a haunting by a 'shadowy male figure' has been connected with Brentwood's martyr William Hunter, who was held here before his execution in 1555.

At the beginning of the century the George and Dragon, on the left (now gone), faces the White Hart, which remains at the time of writing – its Georgian frontage wrapped round an early galleried courtyard at the rear.

The George and Dragon, from the Yard and from the High Street, by A.B. Bamford, early 1890s.

The White Hart Inn from the west, 1912. This inn had for many centuries provided fresh horses and hired out carriages. There was a convenient regular coach to London from here in the early nineteenth century, before the railway took away the traffic. It ran to the Blue Boar in Whitechapel. A daily coach to Bury St Edmunds, useful to farmers, industrialists and commercial travellers, was still continuing to set out from the inn as late as 1848. Stag and foxhound meets started from the yard. In 1848 the inn is also described as housing the excise office.

The Chequers, now demolished, looks across to the Lion and Lamb building, now no longer a public house; both were flourishing at the time of this photograph, *c.* 1910. The Chequers appeared to be of some antiquity. Though the frontage, as usual, had been rebuilt, there was an old panelled ceiling inside in 1891.

The sign of the Yorkshire Grey stands on the edge of the footpath of a quiet and rather primitive-looking top end of the High Street, 1916.

At the bottom, London end, of the High Street, 1915. The old building on the right at the corner of what was Warley Lane but had become King's Road had been the Britannia Beerhouse – a favourite of the soldiers from Warley Barracks. The shop with the blind open is in a building that was once the Seven Stars Inn. This old building had been a private house in 1729. It has been subject to intense but vague phenomena – hauntings and poltergeist activity during the 1950s and '60s. Objects disappeared, a mantleshelf became red hot and noises in the chimney were heard together with shufflings and knockings in a corridor. It is thought these manifestations may be caused by the disturbed spirit of a servant girl who fell down a well in the cellar and was left to rot.

SECTION THREE

BRENTWOOD TOWN

High Street, c. 1910. This photograph includes the Town Hall with its prominent clock: how many shop assistants were made to realize their lateness for work by seeing the time displayed on this? The Town Hall of 1864 replaced the old Assize House and was a sign of Brentwood's growing importance. In postwar days a Courts furniture shop has taken over the site. At the rear was once the market-place, occupying a wide space (now covered with buildings) at the junction of Crown and Hart Streets.

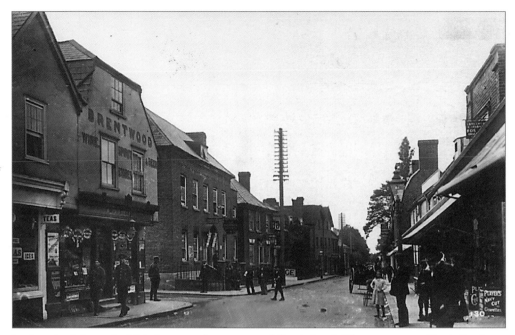

Looking back from the High Street to the junction of King's Road. The entrance to King's Road was considerably widened by the demolition of buildings, particularly the Georgian Cockayne House in the left middle distance, once the home of Brentwood's legendary doctor – Cornelius Butler (1789–1871).

This area at the bottom of the High Street, seen here in 1915, has now been made into a wide junction with the demolition of several properties. King's Road entrance is on the right.

The view past the Town Hall towards London Road, 1920. Some of the farther buildings are still the same as here – though the lower storey has been altered to modern shop fascias.

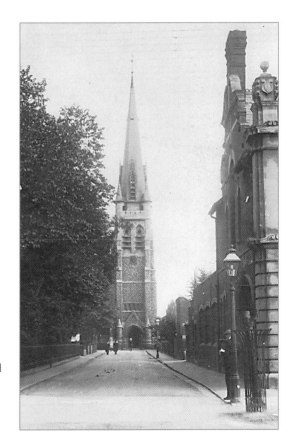

A glimpse of St Thomas's Road, 1910. The old post office on the right was replaced by the present one on the same but enlarged site in 1941. The third St Thomas's Church, in the early Gothic style, was consecrated in 1883.

High Street from the air, *c.* 1930. Various familiar building elevations can be seen in the middle, though others have now changed. The right half of the street is well built-up behind the frontages, but the left side shows a considerable area of open land. This hinterland has now been pressed into service to provide car parking and new roads. Many local trades people have disappeared from the High Street since the 1930s as have Woolworths, the Co-operative Stores and Bon-Marché.

The middle of the High Street, 1905. Many of the shop and inn buildings have a quaint old-world appearance as do the ladies' dresses. Young men stand about on the highway lending the photograph a timeless quality. The pace of commerce would not begin to speed up here until the 1920s. Seen in the middle distance, a familiar sight at this time, are the telegraph poles, an obstruction to the road and footways that would not be tolerated today.

The Ongar Road corner with the High Street, 1929. It is marked by the white building of the new National and Provincial Bank premises. Some splendid motor vehicles have wide spaces in which to manoeuvre, which is just as well as the steering and control mechanisms have some way to go to reach today's standards.

The High Street by Percy Crowe's, 1908. His draper's shops at 52, 54 and 56 High Street were complemented by the house furnishers which he also owned at no. 73 and a tailor and clothier's at Victoria Terrace, Warley Road. Presumably he employed several of his family to help run these diverse ventures. Notice the familiar outline of the two tall buildings with the narrow pavement at mid-left, the profile being very similar today in the Ottakar's bookshop/Dixons area. Only horse-drawn vehicles and bicycles are to be seen. In the mid-distance on the right is the heritage building which has recently been renamed Pepperell House and is now the Information Centre.

At the beginning of the twentieth century saplings were planted midway between the pavement and the road at the Ongar Road end of the High Street, giving a rather curious effect. This photograph dates from 1908.

An exceptionally neat and tidy St Thomas's Road (Queen's Road end), 1906. This eastern side of the road was constructed first, and the tree on the right (or western) side stood between the church and a large piece of open ground behind a paling fence for some time before housing was begun on that side too.

Crown Street was much more suburban in 1910 than today, being lined with villas where people actually lived. These are now either gone or converted into offices. In 1907 James Springett (carrier) at no. 33 Crown Street ran a transport service by horse van to Chelmsford. This operated every Friday, providing Brentwoodians with a cheap and convenient means of conveying bulky items to the county town of Essex. Today car parks occupy much of the space once occupied by quiet and respectable houses and gardens.

Revealing glimpses of the Queens Road/Coptfold Road/St Thomas's Church area from an aeroplane, 1928. Many of the buildings survive today, but some have been replaced by the Chapel High shopping precinct at the top middle of the view. Both sides of the Queens Road end of St Thomas's Road are now built up with solidly constructed houses (bottom of the picture). A large number of the buildings seen here remain today and much of the new construction work has taken place near the top left- and right-hand sides of this photograph, towards Crown Street and the High Street.

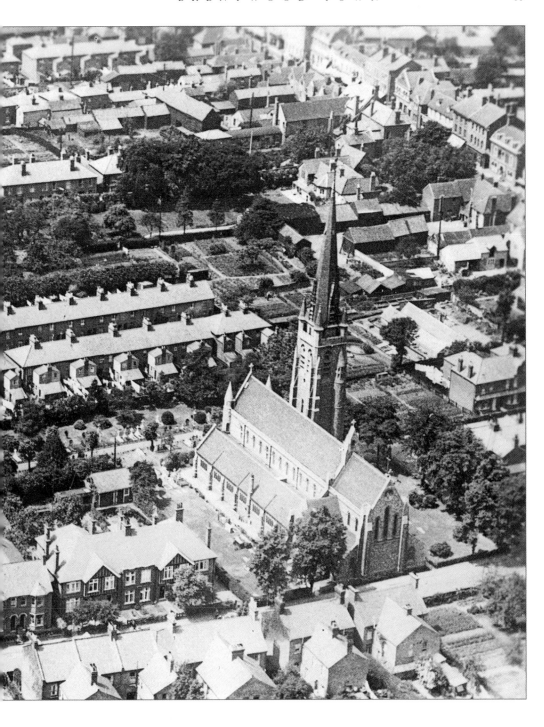

The aftermath of the Great Fire at Wilson's Corner is seen at the middle right of this view, 1909. The conflagration almost completely gutted the premises of this furnishing store which had become a Brentwood landmark, with its high corner tower (complete with clock) erected in 1889. The house nearest the camera became part of Brentwood School, while the house adjacent was eventually incorporated into a rebuilt Wilson's after a forty-year wrangle over compensation.

A later advertisement (1920s) for Wilson's Great Eastern Stores steals a slogan from a famous London department store.

The smouldering skeleton of Wilson's Stores – the would-be firefighters watch the remains after desperately doing their best on 4 September 1909. The outbreak began in a paint store below ground level.

The heat was so intense that even the dummies in the window of J.W. Green's shop across the way at 3 High Street began to wilt, the wax starting to melt in the heat.

The Drill Hall, Ongar Road, stood near where the North Service Road now exits. It was the HQ of the Territorials' Essex Infantry Brigade, which in 1911 consisted of four battalions of the Essex Regiment, including the 4th (Brentwood) Battalion.

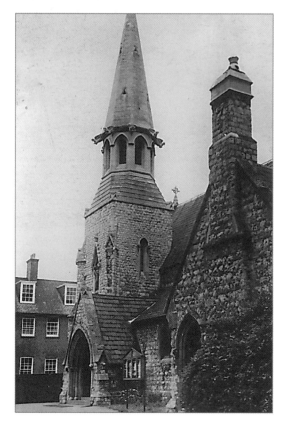

The first version of the Roman Catholic Brentwood Cathedral took over the rather rustic Church of the Sacred Heart and St Helen when the new diocese was formed in 1917.

WARLEY BARRACKS & HOSPITAL AREA

The Duke of York (who would become king in the space of just over a year) with officers at Warley Barracks, 1935. He is maintaining a tradition of royal visits dating back at least to George III, who came to inspect more than 7,000 militia on Warley Common in 1783. They had been gathered together because Britain was thought to be in danger of invasion. The review in October was followed by a mock battle in which 10,000 men took part. In November the camp was dismantled; it was to be reformed again for reviews in 1779, 1781 and 1782.

The entrance to the barracks, *c.* 1904. The buildings are archaic, many dating from about 1805 when the first permanent buildings were built during Napoleonic times. In 1901 the married quarters at Warley Barracks housed 297 out of Great Warley's total population of 1,900.

Soldiers coming off the Parade Ground, Warley Barracks, 1906. When the Napoleonic War ceased in 1815 the Barracks were little used. In 1842 the East India Company bought them, dispatching an annual force of men to India.

A horse and carriage wait outside the gates of the army complex at Warley, 1905. Is the cabman in search of fares? After the Indian Mutiny in 1857 the Crown again took charge of the site.

A military band practising outside the garrison gates, 1913. When regiments marched to and from Brentwood, often on their way abroad or returning from duties there, they were accompanied by a large contingent of bandsmen playing appropriate music.

The Military Hospital, part of the Warley Barracks, 1916. A very necessary provision for such a large army community with families living in quarters and with many new faces passing through on First World War service.

Warley Garrison Chapel, 1920s. At this time the Essex Regiment was the only line regiment to have its own chapel. The chapel had been built by the East India Company for £2,147 to replace the 'riding house' which had been used as an interim place of worship when they took over Warley Garrison in 1842. The chapel survived the demolition of the other parts of the barracks.

The Prince of Wales with his regiment, the Grenadier Guards, leaving Warley Barracks and passing down Warley Road near the hospital gates, 1914. They were to entrain at Brentwood station on their way to Wellington Barracks.

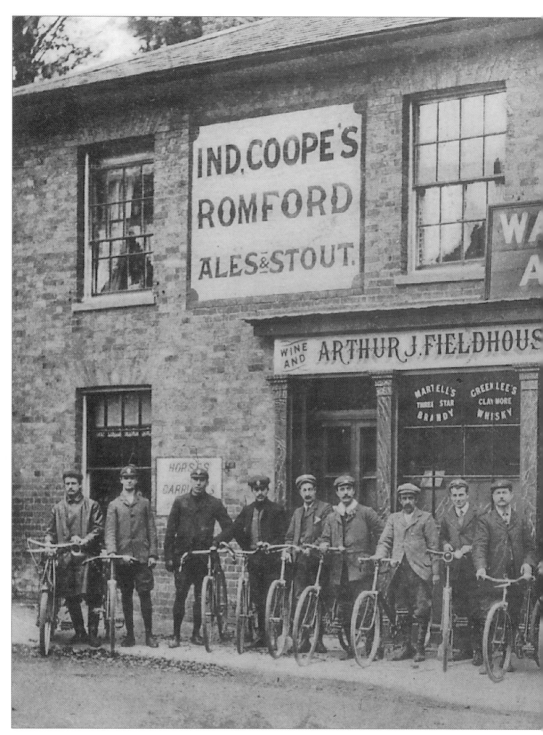

Eighteen members of a Cycling Club meet outside the Warley Arms, probably on a Sunday morning ready to start out on a day's tour of Essex, 1906. Cycling en masse was then an extremely popular hobby throughout the country. Many places of refreshment advertised their willingness to cater for cycling parties en route, displaying the emblem of the Cycle Touring Union or Club, or similar welcoming

slogans. The not fully fit or disabled could also join in, seated in a sidecar. Arthur J. Fieldhouse is listed as the proprietor of the Warley Arms, 159 Warley Road until 1910. By 1912 he had moved to the temperance hotel at 1 Crescent Road.

A glimpse of the principal Warley Hospital buildings, 1905. A hundred acres of the Brentwood Hall Estate were bought from William Kavanagh (after whom the adjoining road is named) in the 1840s for the building of the Essex Lunatic Asylum, which was completed in 1853.

Various businesses served the area around the asylum. Wild's the hairdressers was one of many of that trade, in the early years of the twentieth century. Notice the gaslamp on the left attached to a sewer vent column.

An aerial view of what was now called the Essex Mental Hospital shows the beautiful setting of the institution, *c.* 1929. In the grounds are huge rhododendron bushes, some of which were probably in the grounds of the original Brentwood Hall. This was still being lived in until about 1862 when a remaining portion of the estate was purchased for considerable extensions to the asylum, housing another 500 patients. The main building's architectural style is described as 'Mediaeval . . . of the Tudor period . . . its oriel and bay windows, clock and water towers, turrets, spires, gables . . . give it a most picturesque appearance'. Buildings have been added to the complex until recent times without detracting from the marvellous parkland setting – a great asset to the Brentwood district's charms.

The Warley Road outside the hospital gates has sprouted some early traffic signs, 1914. Along this road at various times would be seen marching columns of soldiers from Warley Barracks on their way to and from the station entraining for exercises in the military arts. Very soon many would be on their way to the real thing – the First World War in France and Belgium, and a great number would not survive.

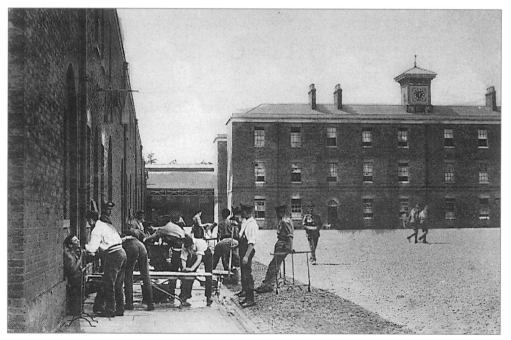

Temporarily off duty at Warley Barracks, 1904. Though much of the accommodation was rather old and therefore spartan, the countryside around the barracks provided a healthy environment for those able to leave barracks.

LITTLE WARLEY & THE STATION

King's Road from the station approach, 1916. Public houses on either side are conveniently placed to refresh the weary traveller alighting from the railway. This area had once been farmland. The bounds of the old Brentwood hamlet ended here at the back of the shops and pub on the right; the boundary roads continued down to the north side of the railway behind the photographer, and along the north side of the railway to Kavanaghs Road, where it ran north.

Queen's Road, 1904. Several Brentwoodians appear to be making their way to the station. The junction with Kings Road is just visible. 'Queen's New Road' was being constructed about eight years after the railway arrived in 1840.

Looking up hill from the Kings Road/Queens Road corner. On the left the garden of the Shrubbery, the house of Colonel Fielder (owner of the small brewery and 'brewery tap' in King's Road), comes to a narrow point. It is now obliterated under a roundabout.

A peep down Rose Valley when trees obscured the view of the houses, *c.* 1906.

A view the other way up the slope of Rose Valley, 1908. This delightful development followed that of Queen's Road, providing commuters with houses conveniently near the new station.

How full of activity is this photograph of 1914. The photographer has his back to the bottom gate of Colonel Fielder's garden and has captured the varied scene in front of him. We can see the houses on the right, now supplanted by offices, although for a period shops existed on the site. There is at this time a surprisingly good shopping area here. In the middle Crosby's, the chemist and druggist, is at 106 King's Road on the corner of Gresham Road, which was constructed at the same time as Rose Valley. Above and

below are many other shops, and services, including boot repairers, coffee-houses, butchers, confectioners, coal merchants, milliners, outfitters, furnishers, dentists, insurance agents, upholsterers, builders' merchants and many private schools. This small area, including Rose Valley, was so self-sufficient that the residents would have had no need ever to visit the High Street or centre of town.

Warley Road, near the station, 1906. Delivery carts and vehicles cluster outside another lively shopping area of the Little Warley suburb. King's Road can be clearly seen in the distance. There is none of the modern clutter of parked vehicles and street furniture to obscure the view.

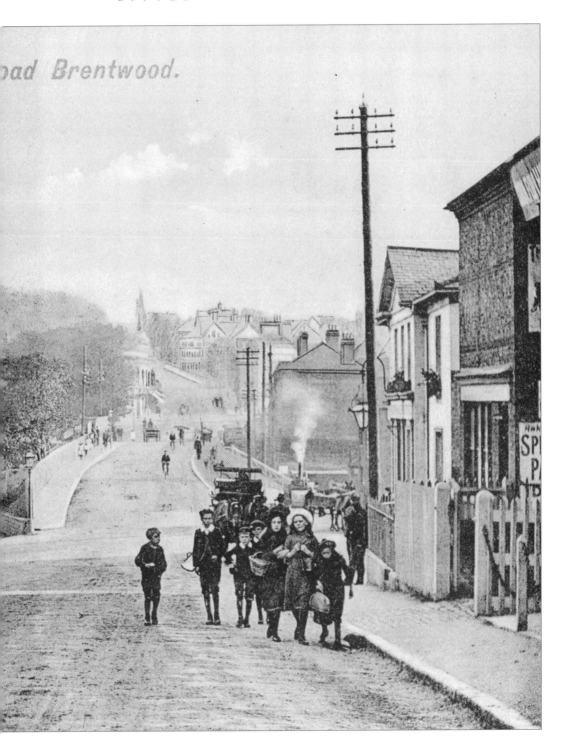

oad Brentwood.

Like many of the people shown in local views of the first three decades of the twentieth century, this smart couple outside their imposing villa in Crescent Road have the appearance of considerable affluence, as evidenced by their clothes and confident stance. Brentwood was generally a 'select' area favoured by those who were 'something in the City' and retired people with good pensions.

Britannia Road, Little Warley, 1908. These houses were built to house the workers at the first Warley factory of Ilford Ltd, photographic plate makers. The houses were red brick, in two terraces and let at 9s a week to employees from about 1904.

Towards the fields and the west end of Westbury Road, these solid houses with several storeys are seen in about 1906. The road was practically finished by 1915. It was to be several decades before any of the roads leading off it would be built.

The King's Road entrance of Westbury Road, 1912. A large house, Westbury Lodge, and its estate had occupied the site in the nineteenth century. The Lodge was 'nicely covered with ivy and wisteria and magnolia trees' – a very Victorian concept. The estate was generous, with a coachman's cottage, a small 'farmery', two fishponds and stabling.

The bend in Westbury Drive, 1920s. Westbury Lodge, which had formerly stood here, had had a fine ground floor entrance, eight large rooms and extensive kitchen and serving quarters. On the upper floor were ten main bedrooms with dressing rooms and servants' quarters. In 1912 a good number of the residents of Westbury Road appear in the selective list of Private Residents published in Kelly's Directory, including the delightfully named Trenhard Calver at no. 73.

SHENFIELD &
BRENTWOOD EAST

Hutton Road corner, 1916. Shenfield developed more slowly than Brentwood proper but a fine row of shops is already in existence at this location. The houses opposite have the dates of construction on the front. Further houses were to be built on the right and later around the corner, where the rebuilding of the old countrified station and bridge together with extra lines of track in the mid-1930s brought a surge in well-built housing and the creation of a busy shopping area around it.

Two views of the Eagle and Child area in early motoring days. Was the vehicle outside in the upper photograph owned by the landlord? In 1909 he was William E. Thurston. The second photograph gives a glimpse of the area to the east of the inn. On the right, part of the premises has been adapted to serve the new motorist's needs. Sited on the old Roman road to Chelmsford, near the junction with the road to Billericay, there was usually plenty of passing trade. None of the later new roads and bypasses leading to the coast and Essex had been built at this early point in the motoring age.

A view the other way towards Hutton Road corner with its post office and the old Green Dragon, *c.* 1908. A haycart adds to the charms of the scene.

A later view of the Green Dragon and the post office, facing east, 1911. Edmund George Platt was the licensee of Ye Old Green Dragon at this time.

Shenfield Rectory, a very Victorian-looking and secluded building, *c.* 1910. At this date the resident of the rectory could regard himself as a country clergyman, living in a farming and mostly rural parish.

Alexander Lane, Shenfield, is still rather tucked away at the edge of things as this view suggests. During the first three decades of the twentieth century the number of houses was added to gradually, but was consistently encouraged by the proximity of the mainline junction railway station.

Shenfield Hall, 1907. Major William Thwaites RA lived at the Hall at this time. In 1887 it was described as 'a fine old mansion'. The Major, however, was not the lord of either of the two manors of Shenfield. In about 1907 Raymond Courage was lord of the manor of Shenfield and lived at Shenfield Place. Philip Townsend of Hatfield Peverell in Essex was Lord of Fitzwaters, this manor house having been destroyed by fire not long before.

Shenfield Road, 1920s. The road still has the curious shut-in feeling with high fences, walls and trees on either side. The strange effect of the telegraph poles with their crowded banks of insulators has gone and so have the wooden rails beside the pavement, which has been improved but is still rather narrow in places.

Under the trees, Shenfield Common, junction of Ingrave Road and Priests Lane, 19 September 1919. The Common underwent a transformation in the nineteenth century. After the railway had been driven through the cutting at the southern end in the early 1840s spoil banks dumped from the building of the cutting created little hills on what had been a flat and low lying section. An old drive led across the common to Thorndon Hall, but when the railway company offered a bridge to keep the drive intact, or money, the Lord Petre of the time accepted the money, and locals pulled down all the trees on the old part of the drive which reached almost to Brentwood.

Peaceful Ongar Road, 1918. The First World War was still raging on the Continent. During the early part of this conflict German airships, generally referred to as Zeppelins, had appeared menacingly over Essex.

Priests Lane was provided with only a very rudimentary footpath in 1904.

Priests Lane funnels into a rather narrow section, 1916. Many of the houses were built at the beginning of the twentieth century with the break-up of the old Glanthams Farm Estate, which stretched a considerable distance from York Road/Hutton Road Junction, Shenfield, past the two bends in Priests Lane to just beyond Glanthams Road. It was sold by J.J. Bassett through the agent A.J. Rippin of 22 High Street, Brentwood. The estate included Worrin Road, Parkway (at first called Park Road), Middleton Road and York Road (originally known as Station Road). Glanthams Road was planned to run on much further across Middleton Road and back again into Worrin Road, according to an early map of the estate.

Near Furzedown, Priests Lane, 1909. The advertising for the Glanthams Estate claimed there were sites to suit purchasers from £2 per foot frontage and that roads were made, kerbed and sewered. The roadway on the left in 1917 bore the scars of a solitary bomb which fell out of the blue, and by great irony killed a nurse who was home on leave from the battlefields of France.

Shenfield Common 'Humps and Dumps', 1912. John W. Larkin wrote in 1906 that 'The Common is a much more pleasant place now', referring to the regulation of the common under a Board of Conservators. Previously it had been in a very poor state. The locals in the nineteenth century did what they liked on it – cutting down trees for firewood, digging gravel in numerous pits which were afterwards abandoned, holding wrestling contests and prize-fights and even badger-baiting. About 1870 what Larkin calls a 'low class of gypsy' were camping on it in dirty canvas tents. 'Hang-dog looking men, and their ill-used women with their poor ill-fed ponies and donkeys, half starved in winter . . . made the Common unsafe in the quiet parts for women or children to walk about on.'

Tranquillity on the Common, 1905. . . . Reflections in the pond.

Cooling off in the Common Pond, which is now railed, summer 1914.

MOVING FORWARD

There were plenty of travellers waiting to catch the incoming train at Brentwood station in the early 1900s. There were only two tracks through the station until 1934. A modernization scheme then gave the section from Romford to Shenfield four tracks. This presented local road operators with their chance to expand their services to keep pace with travel needs. A large number of locals preferred to use the Green Line limited stop luxury coach to get to London in the 1930s.

Eastern Counties' Railway.

OPEN FROM
SHOREDITCH to BRENTWOOD.

THE Public are informed that the TRAINS START from LONDON and from BRENTWOOD, calling at the intermediate Stations of Stratford, Ilford and Romford, at EVERY HOUR, from Eight o'clock in the Morning till Eight o'clock in the Evening, except at the hours of Twelve and One o'clock from London, and One and Two o'clock from Brentwood.

The Ten o'clock, Three o'clock, and Seven o'clock Trains from London, and the Ten o'clock, Twelve o'clock, Four o'clock, and Six o'clock Trains from Brentwood will not call at any of the intermediate stations.

The Five o'clock Train from London will leave first and second class passengers only at the intermediate stations without stopping.

On Sundays the Eleven o'clock and Twelve o'clock Trains do not run; but all the Trains running on Sundays take passengers to and from the intermediate stations.

Coaches are despatched daily by the Trains to Horn-church, Upminster, Ockendon, Billericay, Rayleigh, Southend, Chelmsford, Maldon, Braintree, Halsted, Ingatestone, Witham, Colchester, Harwich, Bury, Sudbury, Ipswich, Norwich, and Yarmouth.

Omnibuses run to and from each train to the Bank, through the Strand and Piccadily, Holborn and Oxford Street, and the new road to the West-end.

Offices, High Street, Shoreditch,
July 17th. 1840.

The great day the Eastern Counties Railway reached Brentwood, 1 July 1840. This notice of a few weeks later explains the times of trains and connecting road coaches. Delays held up the construction of the line beyond Brentwood, so for some time it was only possible to travel in the London direction.

The 'country' side of Brentwood station, *c.* 1900. Note the milk churns awaiting collection and the bell tower on the opposite platform, which informed passengers of the imminent arrival and departure of trains.

Shenfield station, *c*. 1900. While three railwaymen pose for this excellent and detailed view of the station from the bridge, trolleys of goods and luggage await dispatch by train, in the background. The earliest Hutton station on the site was really just a country halt. The first train to reach it through the massive

cutting, which saw several contractors go broke before it was completed, entered it in 1843. The station became more important when it became a junction with the opening of the Southend and new Essex lines to Southminster and Maldon.

Shenfield station, old style, from the outside in Great Eastern days, before the drastic rebuilding of bridge, entrance, track and platforms that was to come in the early 1930s.

The old station approach to Brentwood, *c.* 1908. This is now closed up. A line of shops has been built on to the frontage nearest the camera.

A distant prospect of the seven-arch bridge, September 1927. This has been a favourite subject for photographers over the decades.

Brentwood station: the new station entrances on the bridge in London & North Eastern days, 1930s. The nearest (west side) entry has been closed for many years.

A bus on route 26 bowls down Brentwood High Street, 1923. This service has linked the town with Stratford Broadway since 1921. The route had been introduced by the London General Omnibus Company in 1912 as far as The Unicorn public house, Hare Street, Romford, but withdrawn at the outbreak of the

First World War in 1914. The buildings in the left background, behind the bus, the Lion and the Lamb and the building this side, still retain the same profile in the High Street opposite St Thomas's Chapel and the Georgian house. Note the sign for teas and luncheons nearer the camera on the left.

Another no. 26 descends the hill on London Road, by La Plata, 1920s. Apart from the fact that there is a pavement on the right-hand side of the road, the background scene is similar today. Houses have been built on this end of the La Plata woodland and the police station has been constructed above, but they are well shielded by shrubs and trees from the road. It is hoped that this attractive approach to Brentwood will be retained. After the end of the First World War the 26 bus was reintroduced, running to the west end of Romford (New Mill Inn). Many of the B-type buses had been sent to France during the war to transport troops, and some were abandoned. The bus factory at Walthamstow was soon producing new ones, however, and this enabled an expansion of bus operations leading to the extension of route 26 into Brentwood – one of the farthest outposts of the company in the London area by July 1921.

Ongar Road – the beginning of the motoring age, 1920s. More and more garages were springing up along routes frequented by motorists, often supplying petrol from pumps and via lines which swung out over the pavement. In this picture we can see two motor cyclists, part of a car on the left and signs to do with motor servicing.

Day tourists with their bicycles at the Green Dragon, Shenfield, enjoying the occasion and the country air. The metal sign advertising Pratt's Motor Spirit indicates this was already being mixed with the heady fumes of petrol and scorching rubber.

The vehicles of several competing bus companies ply for trade at the top end of Brentwood High Street, 1930s.

A new bridge has been constructed at Shenfield station as part of the London & North Eastern Railway's modernization scheme of the early 1930s, which involved heavy engineering works practically to rebuild

the track from Romford to Shenfield. Two extra tracks had to be fitted in, through the cuttings and over the bridges between – a real feat of British engineering.

The new street level buildings at Shenfield, mid-1930s. These were designed to cope with the increasing numbers of commuters created by the new streets of housing springing up nearby and the improved facilities for rail travel to London. The shopping parades at the station were also increasingly prosperous, as the process of suburbanization made the area near the station a centre and interchange point between train and bus/taxi/car.

SOUTH WEALD &
BROOK STREET

A familiar view of South Weald village crossroads, 1930s. It is not so dissimilar today for the village has retained much of its rural charm over the centuries. It was the mother parish of Brentwood, which first became a hamlet and then a town. The original parish of South Weald contained three manors. These manors were South Weald, Calcot and Costed, the latter being the one from which mighty Brentwood grew.

Queen Mary's Chapel, South Weald, 1909. This building is connected by local tradition with Mary Tudor, though mainly it has been used as a house, remaining so to this day.

Weald Hall, which was built in the sixteenth century and contained much interesting Tudor brickwork, seen here in 1905. There were elaborate wall paintings of the same period. Unfortunately the house was pulled down in 1950. The beautiful grounds are now a country park.

The Tower Arms, still instantly recognizable, is the village inn of South Weald, and was named after the Tower family who owned Weald Hall. The building, with its red and blue chequer brick front, dates from the eighteenth century.

Wealdcote, 1930s. Said to be a sixteenth-century building, it lies along what was Vicarage Lane but is now Wigley Bush Lane, which is full of delightful architectural discoveries of different centuries.

On horseback by the Bull Inn, Brook Street, 1912. The feeling of a hamlet survives with the retention of the inn and some old cottages. However, there are many new buildings, some of which have detracted from this area – which is full of historical interest. Although the old leper hospital, situated in the area of Spital Lane just beyond the Bull block, has long since gone, two very old buildings can be seen just along the road in the distance – the Golden Fleece inn and the Mary Green Manor Hotel, which had links with the former manor of Brookstreet or Ropers.

Boyles Court, to the north of Brook Street and close to Great Warley, was designed by Thomas Leverton in 1776 in red brick. Bertrand Russell and his wife ran a progressive school here for children before the Second World War.

Buildings near the Golden Fleece at the bottom of Brook Street Hill, 1909. The nearest cottages have been pulled down, but those in the mid-distance survive. In former times the steepish gradient of Brook Street Hill in the centre distance often meant the use of extra horses to get vehicles up the hill. At times wooden blocks had to be inserted under the wheels to stop them running backwards down the hill.

At the top of Brook Street Hill, 1907. The interesting early nineteenth-century 'town' houses are shown.

Serene Honeypot Lane, 1905. Today it is slightly wider, but still winds downhill sinuously.

Rochetts, on the road from South Weald church to Wrights Bridge, from the garden, 1930. A late eighteenth-century brick dwelling, it was successively the home of Sir Thomas Parker, Chief Baron of the Exchequer who died in 1784, and then his famous son-in-law Sir John Jervis, hero of the sea battle of St Vincent. This led to his taking the title Earl St Vincent and to the name of St Vincents Hamlet nearby.

OFF DUTY

Having fun at the Carnival, outside the Old House, 1910. Carnivals in many Essex towns before the First World War served a number of purposes – raising money for charity, particularly the local hospital, fostering community spirit, letting off steam, entertainment before the days of the electronic and canned type. They also gave locals something to look forward to and plan for over the preceding year. In the days of low earnings costumes would be gradually assembled by recycling old garments, paper and cardboard at little cost. Many of the male participants went off to the war in 1914 and did not return. Although attempts were made to resuscitate the event after the end of the conflict it was a long time before spirits revived after the great sadness of so many lost lives.

A stroll with baby – Taskers Lane which became Middleton Hall Lane, 1912.

A family from Ilford enjoy a picnic in the open fields at Shenfield, before the houses came, August 1921.
This day of fresh air and fun was remembered for many years.

A Warley garden party, 1907. In the days before elaborate holidays or trips to the Continent were common, the day's outing with church, Sunday School, women's or men's group or even sometimes from the workplace constituted the main break of the year for many. The venue was chosen carefully to provide the maximum benefits of fresh air, picturesque surroundings and economy of refreshment facilities. During the rest of the year the most was made of family and home-made entertainment. People knew how to enjoy themselves in a simple, unselfconscious way, often lost in today's world.

The Parade at Brentwood station, now replaced by an office block, contained the Parade Cinema, handily placed for the last train home. It is seen here in the 1920s.

The Odeon Cinema in Brentwood High Street, with the gardens adjoining St Thomas's chapel ruins (which are just out of sight). The Chapel High Precinct now starts here.

It is not known where in Brentwood these amateur dramatics are being performed in the 1930s, though the participants are obviously enjoying their parts as much as the audience. Notice the old-style footlights.

The open-air swimming pool was opened in the summer of 1935, and was a tremendously popular facility. Situated in North Road, it closed in 1980.

A small group of cyclists, probably part of a club, has reached the top of the hill into town. They will find several places of refreshment catering for cyclists in the High Street in 1905. All the buildings on the left of this photograph, below what is now Bennetts, funeral furnishers, have now been demolished and a car-park is on the site. The ivy-covered building was up to 1871 a private school run by Francis Monkhouse.

HUTTON

The Chequers Inn, Hutton, 1905. This peaceful rural backwater was to remain so until after the First World War. There being no particular hurry to get anywhere, the owners of the horse-drawn carts have retired inside, out of the heat, for some refreshment that will give them the energy to continue.

Bishops Hill, with the Hutton public house on the right and considerable development of housing visible beyond, 1930s.

Hutton Wash, 1907. The main road here has changed out of all recognition, with houses and shops creating quite a suburban environment by the 1930s.

The beginning of development at Hutton, with the railway cottages at middle and right and the Hutton public house looking towards Shenfield station bridge, 1907. The rail arch over Rayleigh Road was a small one not negotiable by large loads. At this time the station was called Shenfield and Hutton Junction. The state of road surfaces at this time left a lot to be desired – they were to be subject to a gradual improvement as traffic increased over the next few decades.

Hanging Hill Lane, 1930s. At this time it was still a peaceful scene although housing development is beginning to increase along with motor traffic. The winding lane, of which this and the main Rayleigh Road into which it leads are good examples, dates back to very ancient times when such routes were gradually created, as the need arose to avoid difficult terrain such as marsh, steep gradients, and water obstacles. Many of the original difficulties such as water and boggy hazards have long since disappeared, leaving only the bends and kinks in the road to show where they once lay.

The Duchess of York, soon to be Queen Elizabeth (now the Queen Mother), pays a visit to the Child Haven at Hutton, June 1935. She opened a new wing of this home for East End mothers and their children. Seven years before she had opened the first stage of the project, which, 'set amid pleasant sylvan surroundings, provides special treatment for ailing kiddies whose development is retarded by the difficult environment of London's slum-land', as a reporter commented at the time. The new wing for postnatal work had been added because of the high maternal death rate in the poor districts of London.

Looking back along the Shenfield Road from the Green Dragon area, 1914. One of the new road signs promoted by the motoring organizations is on the verge to the right. These were later taken over by the Ministry of Transport. The entrance to Hall Lane is marked by the white house on the right, and Worrin Road on the left by the nearest telephone pole.

GREAT WARLEY

A photograph of the staff of Goldings, the big house at Warley (now the New World Hotel). The occasion is the marriage of Miss Muriel Heseltine to General de Rougemont on 28 May 1914. Evelyn Heseltine, the owner of the Goldings estate, was a great philanthropist to the area, giving £5,000 for the construction of a new church, St Mary the Virgin, next to the house. Dedicated in 1904 and designed by the architect Harrison Townsend, it is known as the 'silver' church, famous for its unique art nouveau decoration which created a silver effect inside.

Partially hidden by the trees is another of Great Warley's big mansions, Coombe Lodge, which has survived. This is a view from the lake.

The dwellings known as the 'Black Huts' at Great Warley provided families with a more economic roof over their head, their cottage gardens producing vegetables to eke out the low domestic budget.

Down Great Warley Street, 1913. White's description of Great Warley in 1848 says it 'is a long, scattered village from 1½ to 3 miles south of Brentwood, and its parish contains 596 souls, and 2,653 acres, 2 rods, 11 perches of land, having a heavy soil on a clay bottom, and giving rise to two sources of the rivulet which flows to Purfleet. It includes Warley Street, Cley Tye and Warley Common.'

The new church of St Mary the Virgin, 1908. Containing unique examples of art nouveau craftsmanship, it was erected by Evelyn Heseltine in memory of his brother Arnold who had died in 1897.

Great Warley Green, 1925. Until this year there was a post office in the village. In 1848 it was located at J. Crossingham's house, and letters were received and dispatched daily via Brentwood.

These children outside Christ Church, Warley, from the Sunday school, are probably dressed up for an outing, 1904. This parish was formed in July 1855 out of portions of Great Warley, Shenfield and South Weald parishes.

'Where sheep may safely graze', Great Warley, 1924. The scene is typical of this rural area.

Highland cattle were popular in this part of Essex at the beginning of the twentieth century.

The rectory, Great Warley, seen from across the fields, 1907.

The Horse and Groom appropriately with horse-drawn transport outside, *c.* 1910. This Victorian pub was the nearest to Warley Barracks, though officially in the parish of South Weald.

The Headley Arms, 1904. It has since been rebuilt in this pleasant setting. The name derives from a previous lord of the manor, Lord Headley, a member of the Allanson-Winn family.

The Thatchers Arms, 1930s. This pub is situated on one of the most prominent corners of the village, on the bend of the main road. The sign is a rare one and the frontage had remained much the same for fifty years. In 1847 James Kerr, described as a victualler, was the landlord. The building is eighteenth century (notice the mansard roof and dormer windows). Up to 1925 the beer at this hostelry was supplied by the Old Hornchurch Brewery. On 3 December 1925 the house was taken over by Mann, Crossman and Paulin, whose sign can be seen. The pub remains today little altered.

HAPPIEST DAYS

Corpus Christi Procession at St Charles School, 1905. The St Charles buildings in Weald Road, once Weald Lane, were Catholic schools run successively by the Brothers of Mercy, the Sisters of Charity and the Irish Christian Brothers from the late nineteenth century up to 1954. From 1971 the site was occupied by the St Charles's treatment centre, until recent closure. The Brentwood area has been a favoured centre for schools of all kinds since the foundation of Brentwood Public School in 1357. Seven 'academies' are mentioned in 1847: Eliza Brown, Martha Carter and Frances Cooper all ran schools in the High Street, while James Monkhouse's Academy was at the top of the hill into the town where the car-park now is below Bennetts. Brentwood School (then known as the Free Grammar) was under the tutelege of the Revds George Tufnell and John H. Bell, Martha Dawson had a school at Broom Well Cottage and the National School was supervized by Thomas Hall and Michael Quin.

Brentwood Public School's newer buildings, 1920s. The wide range of buildings comprising the school, together with its grounds and playing fields, are located on a very large plot. A list of its headmasters dates back to 1568, although the exact dates are not known in one or two earlier cases. Some interesting information can be gleaned from the Statutes, or rules, of 1622 about the school of the time: Scholars were to be at school by 7 o'clock in the morning in winter and 'there to tarry till 11 o'clock in the forenoon'; afternoon school lasted from 1 till 5, but in summer the work began an hour earlier and ended an hour later, from six till six.

The Ursuline Convent dormitories, 1912. The Ursuline School grew out of this establishment. The nuns had been invited to open the school by Canon Morris in 1900 and came from Forest Gate to Matlock, Queens Road, Brentwood from Monday to Friday each week. Initially there were 15 pupils, which increased to 700 later.

Girls in the gym in the more modern school buildings. In 1902 the school moved to 77 Queens Road and later The Grange was taken over and then Belmont. The community continued to grow and lay teachers augmented the teaching staff. The school still exists today and is a substantial establishment.

The buildings of the Ursuline Convent, 1905.

A fierce looking girls' hockey squad, with their sports mistress at the rear, 1912.

The boys' side at the Poplar Schools, 1907. Like most if not all schools in the area, the beginning of the First World War brought requisitioning of the premises and grounds for billeting. The request came on the morning of Saturday 8 August 1914. At midday, 1,000 troops of the 4th Suffolks marched in expecting an empty premises. They immediately took over everything but the residential blocks. In great haste the older girls of the schools were found accommodation elsewhere. After two days the Suffolks went on their way and there was quiet for a few weeks. Then, having assessed the special nature of this billet, the Army brought in the boys from the Duke of York's Military School, Dover. They were destined to stay till 1919 and the end of the war, so the girls and infants were moved to other homes.

The schoolhouse at the front of the Hutton Poplars residential school site, 1930s. The boys from the Duke of York's School, Dover, were nicknamed the 'Dukies'. Dressed in smart red and blue uniforms, the boys included many who were the orphaned sons of soldiers. Four died in the influenza epidemic at the end of the war and were buried at All Saints', Hutton. None of the houses remain, the site having become an estate of new houses, but the school (now part of the Mid-Essex Community College), the gatehouse and the unique boys' dining hall, wonderfully restored by Brentwood Council with its superb roof, tiled decoration and other features, survive.

The girls' side, Poplar School, Hutton, 1907. One hundred acres of land were purchased by the Poplar Guardians, the East End authority, in the early 1900s, in order to provide a better environment for the children in their care. The residential accommodation was arranged around a large green space and the school at the front of the site opened in February 1907. Seven hundred children and babies with their carers were transferred here over two days using the rail service between Forest Gate and Shenfield from their old home. This had been subject to outbreaks of food-poisoning and a bad fire leading to the deaths

of several of the little ones. The move was meant to put this behind them. The fields, woods and country air and the hygienic new premises were a wonderland to many of the youngsters, who had never known these advantages.

Troops were billeted at St Helens School in 1915 and are seen near an entrance. The building formed the original St Helen's Catholic Church of 1837 but became the school in 1861. The site in Ingrave Road was donated by the 11th Lord Petre. The 12th Lord Petre gave substantial amounts to build the second Catholic place of worship – the new Church of the Sacred Heart and St Helen next door. This became the new Brentwood Cathedral when the Catholic diocese was formed in 1912. Since then it has been rebuilt more than once. The latest example is a rather surprising building – a complete redesign standing amid a whole 'village' of Catholic buildings, administrative, educational and sacred.

HERE & THERE

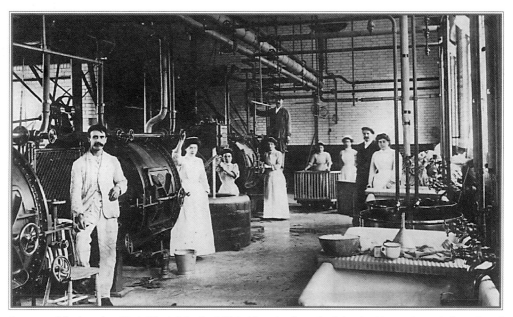

Interior of the laundry, High Wood Schools, 1906. The school was built by the Metropolitan Asylums Board in 1904 to complement High Wood Hospital for children suffering from opthalmia. There five groups of six buildings. By 1930 the patients were children with tuberculosis. There were 240 children still there in 1948 when the Regional Hospital Board took over from the London County Council. The children were moved soon after.

Park Road, once called Beggars Lane, 1906. In late Victorian times Costed Common, between Ongar Road and South Weald Lane, was ripe for development leading to building along the Old Back Lane creating Western Road and Park Road.

Kimpton Avenue, 1908. This road was developed by 1900, as housing began to creep down Ongar Road. Houses were built along the Ongar Road at the end of the nineteenth century and then the land east of this was sold off in lots creating roads such as Kimpton Avenue in the area near the Robin Hood public house.

Robin Hood Road in its early days. It was built in about 1910 on land east of the Ongar Road as Brentwood's development began to gain pace.

Alexandra Road, 1917. This road faced the station – very convenient for railway travel.

The Bungalows, Ingrave Road, 1905. These houses were built along one side of the road with wooded areas facing. They make a contrast with the houses further north.

Hedges, trees and cottage gardens obscure the rural dwellings in this section of Ingrave Road, 1905. This spot was still quiet and rural at this time, although being sited on an important through route to the villages south of Brentwood.

Meanwhile the busy little shop on the main road, Ingrave, caters for both the locals and tourists, on foot or cycle and later in motors, out to see the countryside around Brentwood.

Ingrave village – full of weatherboard houses, hedges and cottage gardens, 1908.

Navestock Church, with its curiously massive timber tower supported on four heavy posts. Together with its interesting monuments (many of the Waldegrave family) and other unusual features, it has been a popular spot with walkers and cyclists since Victorian days.

Blackmore across the pond. It was still being described in about 1938 as a 'hidden village, environed by lovely and undulating landscape'.

Jericho, Blackmore, 1918. Once the site of a priory, which Henry VIII abolished, it was a retreat for the king away from the court. He would sometimes just ride away here, while his courtiers told mystified enquirers that he had 'gone to Jericho'.

The bridge, Blackmore, 1918 – a delight to small children, in this village set in the midst of rich farmland.

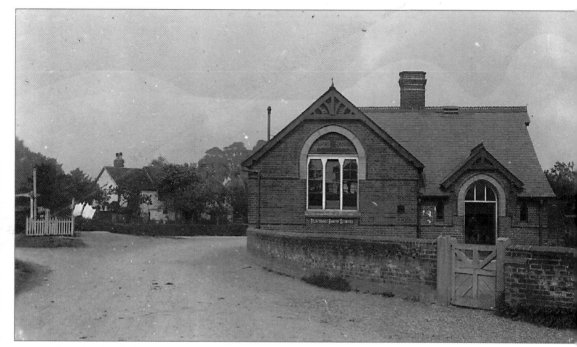

The Schools, Blackmore, 1909. In the late 1920s a blacksmith worked from his shop behind the school, with his little spotted dog and all the children watching before and after schooltime. The farms tended to be mixed, with poultry, pigs, grain, cows and cattle – the farmer's wife looking after the poultry and the income from this side of the activities. Huge shire horses still did all the work of the place until the 1930s, and the cheerful sound of the singing ploughman could be heard in between the rich melodies of birdsong. Things have changed a little now: the blacksmith has departed and there are prosperous commuter homes here.